FOLLOW THE BA

PUBLISHER'S ACKNOWLEDGEMENTS

Acknowledgement is made of grant-aid from the Arts Council of England, Northern Arts, and Rechar (ERDF).

Valuable help has also been received from sponsors. The Principal Sponsor is Northern Rock (see message below), and Co-Sponsors are Alcan Smelting and Power UK and the National Union of Miners (Northumberland Area).

MESSAGE FROM PRINCIPAL SPONSOR

Since 1850, Northern Rock has been offering its communities in the North of England mortgage and saving services. Indeed miners and their families comprised the bedrock of our membership until the 1990s by which time, sadly, almost every pit in the Northumberland and Durham Coalfield had been closed. We are therefore delighted to be the principal sponsors for a new colour version of *Follow the Banner: An illustrated Catalogue of the Northumberland Miners' Banners*, especially as many of our staff have connections with the mining industry.

Whatever our future status, we will continue to offer value for money savings, insurance and mortgage products, and we will also – and with pride and satisfaction – continue to donate a proportion of our profits to charities and other good causes here in our homeland, our beloved North East.

Christopher Sharp CBE
Managing Director
Northern Rock

NORTHERN ROCK

Christopher Sharp died on 8 May 1997. He followed the production of this book with a close personal interest.

FOLLOW THE BANNER

An illustrated catalogue of the Northumberland Miners' Banners

by HAZEL EDWARDS

with a Preface by DAVID WILLIAMS

Mid Northumberland Arts Group
Carcanet Press

For DAVID and THOMAS and ELLA

First published in Great Britain in 1997
by Mid Northumberland Arts Group
Wansbeck Square
Ashington
Northumberland NE63 9XL

in association with

Carcanet Press Ltd
Fourth Floor, Conavon Court
12–16 Blackfriars Street
Manchester M3 5BQ

ISBN 0 904790 95 9 [MidNAG]
ISBN 1 85754 289 4 [Carcanet]
Design & Production, Janet Allan
Set in Palatino by XL Publishing Services, Lurley, Tiverton
Printed and bound in Exeter by
Short Run Press, Exeter

Contents

Illustrations

IN BLACK AND WHITE

IN COLOUR

Preface: Celebration and Protest

Let us not begin with History, for if a few fading survivors of a dying tradition remain somehow bright in the imaginations of Northumbrians that is not explained by the dry recorded facts of date and time of manufacture. Something about these banners stirs the memory and lifts the heart, where history is less potent than nostalgia and the past rises inside you as a chest-vibrating brass band and a full-throated cheer. So let us start with the Picnic. Not a particular Picnic, but the sense of one…

A boy and a balloon squeeze through legs to a precarious perch on the kerbside. Behind, a crowd cranes its neck to peer up the waiting street, swaying forward slightly so that the child steps down into the gutter, back on the kerb, step-step into the gutter. Expectant chat, good-natured banter with a drunk enjoying brief fame as he meanders down the street waving impartially left and right, king and clown for the day. The boy watches him pass, then turns his face up the street again, alerted by the crowd's sudden hush. For a moment all he can hear is the turning of toy windmills. The moment hangs, and is ended by the faraway sound of a big bass drum. The bands are coming. Down into the gutter as the crowd presses on him, and now the child can just see the procession in hoisted squares of bright, moving colour restrained by a sober line of black-and-white in front.

Applause ripples down the street like a stream on either side of the parade. In the middle of the front line someone acknowledges the crowd, waving left and right as the friendly drunk had done. The people all seem to know this man, nudging each other as he comes near enough to be recognized. The boy has seen him too, somewhere – or a picture of him. Sunshine reflects on white shirts at the head of the parade, flashes of silver and gold from the instruments behind.

The first band reaches the child's vantage-point. Last year's winners, pumping through the applause with their best march tune. Miners' fingers working the silver valves – pump, pump, pump. Miners' faces, already glistening with sweat, cheeks red and bulging – polished, like the brass buttons on their red blazers, like their new black shoes marching in time with the drum-beat – thump, thump, thump. The banner follows, red and proud as the band. Gold letters with the name of union and colliery, silver scrolls around a painting of the pit-head outlined against an impossibly blue sky. The poles of the banner have golden spikes pointing up to another impossibly blue sky. Men in Sunday trousers and neatly turned shirt-sleeves keep stout grips on the poles, while others hold the guys like kite-strings.

Bands and banners, banners and bands pass by. Each new beat alters the rhythm of the crowd's applause. As the parade unwinds, spectators at the top of the route start to follow it down to the Picnic field, some walking between the tail-end bands and the lined pavements. The child's eyes dodge past them, searching the patches of colour for a familiar blue-and-black-and-gold. He sees their banner first, and cheers. Somebody ruffles his hair from behind. He turns to pipe above the noise, 'That's them, mam,' and turns again to watch the last band in line. Below the final banner a bandsman has perched his hat on top of his big bass drum. The hat jumps at every beat. The boy calls out to his dad, who looks sideways for a second, bareheaded and breathless, to grin at his son. Then, with renewed vigour, he strikes the drum, beating time for the band and the army of picnickers following the parade. The boy and his mam tuck in behind the banner and march with the drum to the Picnic field for contests, speeches and toffee apples...

The crowds streaming behind the banners at the Picnic were an uplifting sight. Better still was to be part of that river of people whose high-day spirits were perfectly expressed by the warm, confident, slightly vulgar tones of the brass band and the bold display of gaudy banners, their own emblems of pride in and loyalty to their community.

Of course the parade behind the banner has not always been a cheerful procession or one with celebration as its purpose, nor has the sight of it always gladdened the hearts of such as mine-owners and Government. The story of the miners' banner is a political one, with blood on its pages. Struggle and defiance were the warp and weft of early banners, made for the great Chartist gatherings of the 1830s and quickly adopted by the trade unions for their own demonstrations. The report of a mass meeting in 1831 was the first record of their use by miners: 'A large meeting of miners was held at Jarrow, each colliery bearing a banner with the name of the colliery and various mottoes.' The urge to stand up and be counted – to be identified with the struggle – is already there in that brief account. Later in the same year a mass meeting of the miners of Northumberland and Durham was held on Boldon Fell, near Sunderland: 'The roads in the vicinity of the meeting-place presented an unusual bustle, the men walking in procession from the different collieries bearing flags and banners and accompanied by bands...'

Banners and bands: they were an identity tag, a rallying-cry and a gesture of defiance. Even the orderly nature of the meetings represented a threat to the authorities, for a disciplined force that assembled under its own flags could be infinitely more dangerous than a rabble, especially in such large numbers. And the numbers were growing. During the great strike of 1844 around 30,000 men collected on Newcastle Town Moor and seventy-two banners were counted that day. According to Richard Fynes, 'Nothing could be more imposing than the sight of the men marching in procession as they came to the Town Moor.'

Thus emerged the pattern of protest that would endure over the next century, through the bitter conflicts between miner and coal-owner and latterly the NCB. As their own history developed, banners became not merely statements for their time, but emblems of continuity that linked the 'long strike' of 1887 and the General Strike of 1926 and the grinding dispute of 1984 and 1985. They provided pitmen with a connecting thread to past struggles and a sense of tradition that gave strength, purpose and character to their own fights.

The miners' story was woven into their banners over the years, the motifs and mottoes changing to echo contemporary conditions and challenges. Early themes were the right to vote, the demand to have mines inspected and regulated, and to have disputes settled by arbitration. As the century turned the banners called for better working conditions and terms of employment, and for nationalization. One banner from the Ashington group of collieries in the 1930s made 'A Plea for Nationalization' and showed a worker as St George armed with a spear of 'State control' slaying the dragon of 'profit and private ownership'. These were messages to the outside world; the miners themselves were urged to organize, unite and be proud. The Newbiggin (later Lynemouth) Branch banner exhorted its members in bold capitals:

PERFECT YOUR ORGANISATION:
EDUCATE YOUR FELLOWS: LOOK TO THE REGISTER
SPREAD THE LIGHT – AND THE FUTURE IS YOURS

Remarkably – even in the harshest of times for the miners and their families – no hatred was ever expressed in their banners. The images were vivid and the words often passionate, but never malevolent. Banners were characteristically affirmative rather than negative. Deprivation and sorrow were potent themes and all too appropriate, yet rarely employed. A recurring subject was the widow grieving over the loss of her husband, but it was not typical. Optimism, fortitude and faith in the future were the qualities most often expressed in mottoes, slogans and illustrations.

There is something more behind this way of confronting the world than a legacy of the Victorian belief in the virtues of self-help, or the influence of non-conformist religious principles, though these played their part in establishing the imagery and language through which attitudes were declared. Anyone who has lived for long in a straitened but close-knit mining village knows that hope and high spirits are the natural resources of a community whose positive life-force expels bitterness and despondency. It is above all an innocent community, with a deliberately circumscribed world view that shields it from misanthropy and cynicism. If it takes a Sunday School view of social, political and moral issues that has less to do with the influence of chapel than with the ingenuousness that is its strength and protection.

Appropriately, then, picture parables and biblical homilies were often the chosen agents of communication, first by the local artist, signwriter, talented branch member who were the early banner-makers and later by firms such as Bainbridges of Newcastle who made a business out of growing demand and offered stock designs and quotations to suit the needs of a particular Lodge.

Prince among the manufacturers was George Tutill, showman by nature and occupation, whose banner-making business in London established by the end of the nineteenth century a virtual monopoly and an unsurpassed reputation. Tutill's habit of offering substantial discounts to customers who chose one of his standard designs has been criticized for stultifying development – and it is true that many standard designs being offered in the 1890s were still available in 1930 – but the criticism under-estimates the importance of tradition and continuity in the art and in the history of the trade union movement. Nor should Tutill's pragmatic commercial approach blind us to his true qualities as an artist for the people. His early experiences as a travelling showman led him to develop a popular fairground art which strongly influenced the design styles of banners far beyond his own time. He eschewed the abstract or otherwise indirect art forms requiring mediation or interpretation in favour of direct communication through a strong emphasis on the pictorial, the precise representation. At the same time his images were stylized, sentimentalized, so that they were at once familiar and elevated, humanity reaching beyond its condition. It was an immediate and powerful message.

Nowhere was the message more powerful or better-received than in the parade of banners at Northumberland Miners' Picnic, where political meeting merged with family festival and protest was translated into celebration. The first Picnic was held at Polly's Folly in a field between Boghouses and Shankhouse in June 1866, and it quickly established itself as an annual occasion. Carlisle Park, Morpeth was its home during the 1920s and 1930s, Bedlington in later years, and it has also been staged in Ashington, Newbiggin and on Blyth Links. In 1919 the union held a Western Picnic at Hexham and it was intended to have two Picnics every year thereafter, but Hexham Council refused a second gathering in 1920 on the grounds that it was a socialist demonstration.

Today the nostalgic appeal of this gala is such that a lively discussion can be provoked among older residents in any Northumberland pit village by asking which was the ideal venue for the Picnic. Opinions differ, but whatever the location it is certain that for many years the event was the highlight of a calendar with few enough red-letter days for miners and their families. In the bleak 1920s and 1930s it often provided their only opportunity during the year to leave the village for a holiday. In those days almost the entire community would march behind its band and its banner from the village to the Picnic site. Parties from more distant villages would travel in great excitement by train or bus. The atmosphere was unequalled, charged by a carnival spirit of occasion and release, heightened by the friendly but intense rivalry between collieries competing for best band and banner on parade, fuelled by the rhetoric of guest political speakers whose heightened emotive levels were their own response to the mood and energy of the festival.

The list of speakers over the years at the Picnic would read like a roll of honour were there not some fallen angels among the heroes of the movement: Ramsay MacDonald, Manny Shinwell, Sir Stafford Cripps, Ellen Wilkinson, Clement Attlee, Nye Bevan, Hugh Gaitskell, Harold Wilson, Michael Foot and Neil Kinnock among others. Many of these names and faces achieved immortality in the banners too; some of the finest examples of the art have been stunning portraits of these leaders. Miners expect their heroes to remain steadfast, however – the 'treachery' of Ramsay MacDonald and Philip Snowden led to their banner images being excised, painted over or otherwise besmirched. Chief among the revered was Keir Hardie. 'His vision was our inspiration', declared the banner of West Sleekburn miners below his beautifully executed portrait.

The parade at the Miners' Picnic was a dynamic history and moving gallery of these wonderful pictures and legends, the old lining up with the new, Tutill's famous designs alongside the work of homegrown artists such as Oliver Kilbourn. But if this proud procession represented the glory of the mining industry and its trade union movement, so it also marked its gradual decline as the dwindling number of banners raised at the Picnic reflected the harsh facts of pit closures. In 1950 the Northumberland Miners' Union had fifty-eight Lodges, with up to thirty banners at the Picnic. By 1980 there were only eleven Lodges and seven banners. A decade later the Northumberland coalfield was moribund.

When the last great strike was ended and the miners returned to work, they did so, not with an air of defeat, but marching behind their bands and banners. The battle may have been lost, but their spirits had been put to the severest test and found true. Many knew in their hearts that this was their last hurrah, but they were equally aware that they had written a new page in the history of the working classes and provided inspiration for struggles yet to be joined, in other places, other times. It was with courage, with justice and with pride that they raised their banners in celebration.

DAVID WILLIAMS

1 Follow the banner: *an introduction*

What is the appeal of banners? They inspire awe and affection amongst people both inside and outside the labour movement. They are theatrical: their brilliant colours of red, blue, gold and silver combine with their improbable size to create a dramatic presence at a meeting or procession. They just cannot be ignored. Their fine illustrations and stirring slogans are devices borrowed from the world of fairground showmanship and commercial art, yet their messages have a deeper resonance. They promote the benefits of union membership and proclaim a pride in industrial skill and labour. They recall past struggles and victories in union history, remind us of goals still to be won and those already won but which today's trade unionists are having to reclaim.

For the six men carrying the lodge banner and their comrades marching behind, it is their rallying point, their battle standard. Throughout the history of union banners, the miners have undoubtedly been the chief banner bearers. The dangerous nature of their work and the cruel injustices dealt out by coal-owners have meant that their struggle for improved wages, safety and welfare has been particularly bitter. Their struggle has not been confined to the workplace; entire communities have been caught up in pit disasters, demonstrations, evictions and strikes. And perhaps because of this involvement, miners' banners have become important expressions of *community* identity and solidarity.

It has only been in the past two decades that historians, museum curators and trade unionists have come to recognize the value of banners as evidence of union history. This awakening is very much due to the pioneering work of the late John Gorman, who travelled the country rescuing long-forgotten banners from the attics and cellars of welfare clubs, halls and pubs. In 1973 he published the results of his research in a book called *Banner Bright* (republished in 1986).

Drawing on this seminal work, *Follow the Banner* contains an illustrated catalogue of the twenty surviving banners of the Northumberland coalfield, most of which are now held by Woodhorn Colliery Museum in Ashington. The catalogue analyses the imagery and slogans of each banner and provides insights into their history gleaned from the handwritten pages of branch minute-books. Before each banner is examined, the Northumberland collection is discussed within the context of the banner tradition which spans 170 years and which is shared by trade unionists across the country.

2 Unfurling the banner: *the emergence of the trade union banner*

Inevitably the history of banners is intertwined with the growth of the trade union movement. The first trade-union banners were flown in the early nineteenth century. As Britain industrialized in the eighteenth and nineteenth centuries, a new breed of skilled workers began to organize themselves into trade societies or unions. They drew on the ritual and regalia of the craft guilds of the medieval age, the secret societies of Freemasonry and religious dissent of later times. During the years of the Combination Acts, 1799–1824, when unions were illegal, public demonstrations of association such as the parading of banners were impossible. In 1825, however, the Combination Acts were abolished, trade union membership became legal and the banner tradition began.

A cartoon of the Northumberland and Durham miners' union of 1832. The pitmen march behind their leader, Thomas Hepburn (in black), carrying flags with slogans supporting their cause.

According to Richard Fynes's account of the Northumberland and Durham miners, first published in 1873, banners were carried by the North East pitmen as early as 1831. At this time the miners of Northumberland and Durham joined other working men in the agitation for the reform of political and industrial inequities. In 1830 their leader, Thomas Hepburn (1785–1864), formed the first Northumberland and Durham miners' union. Although the union foundered in 1832 at the end of a six-month strike, the tradition of flying banners had been established amongst the miners of the North East. Fynes, in his description of the strike of 1844, counted seventy-two banners present at a meeting on Newcastle Town Moor.

These early banners, as Fynes observes, were probably hastily prepared by a union member or local sign-writer. They carried demands for immediate action, unlike the later elaborate silk banners which bore dignified statements of solidarity, industrial pride and mutual aid. By the 1850s the first New

Model unions for the skilled industrial workers began to emerge and a man called George Tutill had established a flourishing business making silk banners. The parading of union banners had become an accepted feature of public life. Indeed in 1864 the Northumberland miners formed their own countywide union, and in the following year they expressed their solidarity at a mass meeting at Blyth. This meeting soon became an annual event known as the 'Miners' Pic-nic' and parading banners became an integral part of the day's proceedings.

The parading of banners was at its height in the last decade of the nineteenth century. Thousands were commissioned by lodges of the new and very powerful general unions which represented whole industries, such as the Miners' Federation of Great Britain founded in 1889. And it was not just trade unionists who carried banners. Members of Friendly Societies, temperance groups, Co-operative Societies, Orange orders, churches, chapels and Sunday schools all took to the streets bearing their billowing silken banners. In the 1920s a new militancy, inspired by the Russian Revolution of 1917, the terrible experiences of the Great War (1914–18), and an increase in union membership, led to the commissioning of another wave of trade-union banners with confident demands for change. The failure, however, of the General Strike of 1926 dealt a severe blow to this confidence and trade-union orders of Tutill banners dwindled.

Although the making and parading of banners is essentially a late Victorian phenomenon, the post-war election of 1945, when the first majority Labour government was elected, gave rise to a new generation of banners which celebrated Labour's triumph. The miners participated in this banner resurgence with particular enthusiasm, commissioning new banners to proclaim the nationalization of their industry in 1947. The defeat of the Labour government in 1951, however, led to a slowdown in the commissioning of new banners by union branches. Their memberships declined in the following decades due to the erosion of heavy industry, unemployment and the increase in casual, non-union labour. This decline, as John Gorman writes in *Banner Bright*, can be charted in the order books of the George Tutill banner-making company. In 1967 the company, for the first time in its history, received no orders from trade unions. In the Northumberland coalfield the Annual Picnic sustained the tradition but the number of banners dwindled as pit after pit was closed during the 1960s, 1970s and 1980s. The 1984–5 miners' strike and the Campaign Against Pit Closures of 1992 gave rise to brief revivals which encouraged the restoration of old banners and the commissioning of new ones, but the rallies at which they were flown were never the vast spectacles of a century earlier.

3 The banner message: *design and imagery*

The fortunes of the trade union movement not only determined the number of banners in existence but also contributed to the messages they carried. Although eighteen of the twenty surviving Northumberland miners' banners were inspired by the euphoria of Labour's 1945 victory, the collection as a whole illustrates many of the recurrent themes of trade-union banners.

Their layout and design has remained consistent during the past 170 years and this is due to the monopoly George Tutill had on the banner market and the way other banner-makers tended to imitate the Tutill style. Early trade unionists wanted to proclaim the medieval origin of their skilled trade, so the standard banner comprises a central picture presented like a shield or heraldic coat of arms. The elaborate renaissance-style gilt scroll work and foliage which fills the background is, in contrast, a product of the Victorian obsession with ornamentation. The painted scrolls or ribbons which ripple across the top and bottom of the banners carry the lodge name and slogan.

The central pictures are usually painted in a style described by Anthony Lewery in *Popular Art Past and Present* as 'academic art' which, though competent, sometimes lacks the qualities of true naturalistic painting. Some of the Northumberland banners which were not products of the prestigious Tutill studios were painted in a more naïve style which has its own particular charm, for example, the banners of Ellington, Doctor Pit, Lynemouth, Seghill, Whittle and Woodhorn. Some art critics, such as Lewery and Emmanuel Cooper, believe these banners exemplify folk or popular art. Instead of looking at them from a purely aesthetic or high-art perspective, they prefer to view them within the context in which they are produced, that is, the home or the workplace. In truth, the examples from the Northumberland collection are either the work of a second-rate banner-maker (this applies to the Doctor Pit [11], Lynemouth [15] and Seghill [23] banners) or a melding of commercial and folk art. The Whittle and Woodhorn banners [26, 27] were the products of partnerships between amateur painters, who designed the imagery, and professional banner artists who painted the designs directly on to the silk. The Ellington banner [13, 14], however, is in a different league. The professional banner artist worked from an original design painted by the acclaimed pitman artist, Oliver Kilbourn. The resulting banner is very traditional in format but contains detail which only someone with an intimate knowledge of mining culture could portray.

The earliest trade-union banners, as already mentioned, were heavily influenced by the heraldry of medieval craft guilds and also the imagery of nineteenth century Friendly Societies. Indeed, in the early days unions were virtually indistinguishable from the latter, for welfare and security were their main concerns. Although commissioned much later, the North Walbottle banner [18,19], made by Tutill, provides a fine example of this influence. It was originally designed as the arms of order for a Friendly Society and is highly complex, crowded with symbols ranging from female classical allegorical figures to biblical references and the all-seeing eye borrowed by Friendly Societies from Freemasonry imagery. The overall impression is one of respectability which is reinforced by the conciliatory motto: 'Let brotherly love continue'.

In stark contrast is the banner of the Ashington Group of Collieries [1, 2], made in the 1920s which conveyed a clear message of defiance. It reflects the way trade unions of the late nineteenth century had abandoned their protectionist, moderate, self-help role in favour of a more class conscious, anti-capitalist position. Not unlike the North Walbottle banner, it carries a profusion of images but rather than being selected for their individual symbolic meaning they illustrate a narrative. The reverse makes an impassioned 'Plea for Nationalization', while the front of the banner demands all workers to unite and evokes the popular vision of a co-operative commonwealth as their reward for unity. Like several other of Tutill's standard catalogue designs, this image draws on an illustration by the socialist artist, Walter Crane (1845–1915). The rural idyll it presents is a popular motif on other banners including Lynemouth [15], and also on the Bomarsund [6, 7] and Ellington banners where it is translated into the suburban Garden City. Portraits of local and national union leaders and Labour politicians began to appear on late nineteenth-century union banners and the miners enthusiastically embraced this trend. In fact five of the Northumberland miners' banners bear portraits of their heroes. The miners understood where the real power lay, and the Houses of Parliament adorn four of the Northumberland banners.

Between the 1890s and the 1930s Tutill's designs fossilized. It took the Labour victory of 1945 to invigorate banner design, and nationalization of the coal industry in 1947 is the dominant theme of half of the eighteen Northumberland banners commissioned in the post-war period. The optimism of this time is symbolized on several of the Northumberland banners by a rising sun or the warm glow of dawn. Another theme common to most of these later banners is the pride the miners felt in their industry. It is expressed in the detailed depictions of the tools, machinery, underground pit scenes and surface buildings. This pride in their labour, skill and industry was undoubtedly engendered by the sense of ownership the miners felt following nationalization, but it also reflects a tradition which can be traced back to the earliest banners of the skilled industrial workers.

Taken together, the Northumberland banners demonstrate how banner-makers over the past 170 years remained loyal to the original format whilst changing the themes and style of the central emblems. The highly detailed banners of the late nineteenth century and early twentieth century, typified by North Walbottle and Ashington Group of Collieries, were never matched. Most post-war banners, even those made by Tutill's company, do not display the detail and craftsmanship of their forerunners. Their designs are more simplistic and rely on motto and symbol to convey their message. In many ways banner design has come full circle, returning to the simple slogan banners carried by the North East pitmen during the strikes of the 1830s and 1844. Workers fighting for the right to form a union in the early decades of the nineteenth century, or the trade unionists of the 1980s and 1990s fighting for the very survival of their industries and unions, can ill afford an elaborate banner laden with subtle imagery and historical references. Their banners must be readily understood and convey persuasive demands for immediate action.

4 The banner-makers: *George Tutill and his imitators*

It is questionable whether the banner tradition would have been as vibrant and enduring without the vision and energy of the Victorian entrepreneur, George Tutill. He was born in 1817, the son of an illiterate Yorkshire miller, but when he died in 1887 production at his banner-making company was at its height. Over a century later, his company is still in business trading under the name of George Tutill Limited, in Chesham, Buckinghamshire and, since the late 1970s, in association with the well-established banner-making firm of Turtle and Pearce Limited in Southwark, London. (The history of this remarkable man was uncovered by John Gorman and a full account can be found in *Banner Bright*.)

Over three-quarters of all the trade union banners made from 1837 onwards were products of the Tutill banner-making empire. Six of the surviving Northumberland miners' banners carry the Tutill signature and a further four, although not 'signed', display the imagery and quality usually associated with a Tutill banner. Furthermore, it is safe to assume that many of the historic Northumberland banners were also made by his company. The story of George Tutill is therefore integral to the history of the Northumberland

Banner artists at work in the George Tutill studios in 1935.

miners' banners. As Gorman discovered, Tutill probably began his working life as a travelling fairground showman. The similarities between the fascias of fairground sideshows and nineteenth-century banners demonstrate the impact Tutill's early working experiences had on banner art. In 1837, at the young age of twenty, Tutill founded his banner-making business.

All Tutill's banners were made of a single square or rectangle of pure silk, and in 1859 he chose to locate his business at 83 City Road in order to exploit London's East End silk-weavers. They were descendants of the French Protestant Huguenot weavers who settled in Spitalfields from the 1680s onwards. (The Tutill business was moved to Chesham in Buckinghamshire following the bombing of the City Road premises in 1940.) Tutill offered his clients two types of silk banner. The cheaper plain woven silk squares had backgrounds of elaborate foliage and scroll work *painted* in gold or silver, while the ornate surrounds of the more expensive banners were *woven* into the silk on an enormous Jacquard loom installed in the City Road premises in the 1880s. (Two of the surviving Northumberland banners, Ashington Group and North Walbottle, were products of this Jacquard loom.) These woven damask silk banners were unique to Tutill, and in order to protect his company from competition he took out a patent. He also patented his India rubber and linseed oil treatment of silk banners which rendered their oil-painted centres pliable and very durable.

The banners were painted by a team of talented artists. The 'corner men' were responsible for the elaborate surrounds, other artists specialized in portraits, technical or architectural subjects, and the general artists painted the landscapes and emblems. No banner was complete without the lodge name and slogan, skilfully painted by a signwriter. Tutill's service did not end with the production of a banner: he supplied lodges with carrying poles, tassels, silk cord, guide tapes, and a solid wooden box in which to store the furled banner. Full details of Tutill's services were advertised in a catalogue but sadly only a few copies of the 1895 and 1930 editions survive today.

The recurrence of certain mottoes and imagery on Tutill banners can be attributed to the way he encouraged lodges to select their banner from the standard designs presented in his catalogue. The banners representing the Ashington Group of Collieries and North Walbottle are both standard catalogue designs. It was of course possible for branches to commission a unique design based on a photograph or sketch, but this cost more. Examples of specially commissioned designs from the Northumberland collection include the colliery building depicted on the Rising Sun banner [22] and the Bomarsund and Sleekburn 'A' banners [24] which were based on sketches by a local man. It is clear from the banner designs offered in the catalogue and from the numerous testimonials from satisfied customers that Tutill supplied banners to more than trade unions. Organizations as diverse as Druid orders, Sunday schools, temperance leagues and Orange orders patronized George Tutill.

George Tutill was not the sole banner-maker in Britain and some of the Northumberland miners' lodges chose to place their orders with other manufacturers. The fine Pegswood banner [20, 21] which celebrates nationalization so vividly was made by the Birmingham regalia company of Fattorini, while the second, and possibly the original, Ellington banner was made by the famous regalia firm of Toye, Kenning and Spencer. Unfortunately the makers of other Northumberland banners are unknown.

5 The banner men: *purchasing and parading the lodge banner*

The flying of huge illustrated banners, as John Gorman observes in *Banner Bright*, is unique to British trade unions (although in due course it was taken up by trade unions in British colonies). Within the coal industry, the tradition of purchasing and parading a banner is strongest at the branch or lodge level. Fascinating rituals surround the commissioning, unfurling and carrying of a colliery banner and they are often recorded in meticulous detail in the branch minute-book.

Considerable competition existed amongst lodges and the acquisition of a banner, particularly a Tutill banner, signalled the 'coming of age' of a branch. A banner represented a considerable financial investment and the decision to purchase one was not taken lightly by the committee men, who often consulted the whole membership at the Annual General Meeting (AGM). According to the Tutill catalogue of 1895 a basic painted silk banner, twelve feet by ten feet, cost 23 guineas and 4 guineas extra for a woven banner. By the 1930s prices for similar sized banners had only increased to about 70 pounds. In 1949 Sleekburn 'A' lodge was quoted £110-10-0 for a Tutill banner, but by the early 1980s costs had risen sharply and in 1982 Ellington branch probably paid Toye, Kenning and Spencer Limited in the region of £3,000 for a copy of the original 1950s' silk banner. Few branches had enough surplus money to cover such sums, so they usually established a 'banner fund' and set about raising money in a variety of ways.

In 1950–1 the branch members at Ellington organized dances and a Christmas draw to help pay for their new banner. Yet, according to the minutes of the committee meeting held a day after the banner's first outing at the Annual Miners' Picnic, the branch was still out of pocket. The committee men, therefore, agreed to ask branch members to pay two levies of six pence. They also rejected an appeal for funds from the local Labour Party in view of the 'financial position due to the purchase of the banner'. If a branch was short of funds, it would often adopt a banner from a neighbouring pit which had been closed and the old branch name would be overpainted. This recycling of a redundant banner occurred at Lynemouth [15] with the adoption of the old Newbiggin banner and at Whittle [26] when the lodge was offered the former Pegswood banner.

Once funds had been secured, the branch committee had to select the design. Often it was merely a matter of choosing an appropriate combination of emblems and mottoes from the Tutill catalogue. Occasionally a banner design was the result of a competition, as with Woodhorn's and Whittle's, or a local artist was asked to come up with some sketches. Sometimes, due to a lack of funds, affection for the old design, inertia on the part of the branch officials or a combination of all three, a branch would commission a repeat of the old banner. The banner carried by the Ellington miners is an exact copy of the original 1950s' banner designed by the pitman painter, Oliver Kilbourn, and there are three versions of the Ashington Federation banner which features the five local collieries.

A framed certificate hangs in the NUM office at Ellington Colliery; it records the dedication and blessing of the aforementioned lodge banner by the Industrial Chaplain of the North East coalfield during the 1982 Annual Miners' Picnic. Elaborate ceremonies such as this often accompanied the official unfurling of a new banner. These occasions were more likely to occur a few weeks before the Annual Miners' Picnic rather than on the day. They took place in the Welfare Institute or Social Club and were attended by local and regional union officials and the colliery manager. After the banner had been formally unfurled it was often carried through the streets, led by the colliery band, so that the wider public could view it, thus reinforcing its role as an expression of *community* pride and identity. Branch minute-books reveal that other occasions when banners were paraded were quite numerous. Some events were of a political nature such as May Day demonstrations, Labour Party rallies, or the 1926 General Strike meeting addressed by A.J. Cook in Ashington and attended by the Ashington Federation banner. Other gatherings had a family or community flavour, such as the Hospital Sunday procession which the Ashington Federation banner joined in February 1927, or Lynemouth's Children's Gala of 1951 at which the Ellington banner was present. Occasionally the lodge banner, draped in black crepe, would fly at the funeral of a union luminary or the victim of a pit accident. But the big occasion at which *all* the Northumberland miners' banners would be flying was, of course, the Annual Miners' Picnic.

The Miners' Picnic has a long history: records show that the earliest Picnic was in September 1863 at Blyth. It became an annual event which has taken place every summer except during the First and Second World Wars, and the miners' strikes of 1921, 1926 and 1984–5. Blyth Links was a frequent location for the Picnic in the early days whilst Carlisle Park in Morpeth became its home in the 1920s to the 40s. Although it was staged in Ashington on four occasions, from the 1950s until 1992 Bedlington was the home of the Picnic.

As David Williams remarks in the Preface, the Picnic is a unique combination of protest and celebration: it is both a political meeting and a family day out. The day has a well-established format of which the banners are an integral part. In the early morning the banner and colliery band assemble and parade through the streets of the pit village before travelling to the site of the Picnic. Throughout the day the banner is the responsibility of six 'banner men' (two pole men and four ribbon men). They are usually elected at the branch AGM and are paid the equivalent of a shift's earnings. A brass band contest is staged in the morning and the banners, anchored to lamp-posts, fly above the spectators. At midday the Picnic procession moves off, headed by union leaders and Labour politicians. Each colliery is represented by its banner and brass band and the miners and their families fall in behind. At the Picnic field the assembled throng listens to speeches by the Labour leaders; they sit amongst cornets and trombones abandoned by the bandsmen who hastily depart for the club or pub. The banners provide the backdrop; attached to fence-posts they mark the boundary of the Picnic field. With the speeches over and the band contest results announced, the procession reassembles to march back into town. This is the end of the formal part of the day – the fair-ground and social club beckon – and the banner is returned to its box or wrapped around the poles. At the time of writing, the recent Picnics have taken place at Woodhorn Colliery Museum, but the future of this day is now in question, with only one deep mine left in the North East coalfield.

6 Furling the banner: *the decline of a tradition*

Banners are fragile. Although silk is surprisingly robust, a standard banner, buffeted by the wind, soaked by rain and tainted by mildew, is unlikely to survive unscathed. In fact, many branch minute-books record how banners were returned to their makers for repairs. Arguably, they are not designed to last. They are ephemeral; their portraits and slogans become dated and new banners are commissioned whilst the old ones are destroyed or left to lie, forgotten and rotting, in the loft of a branch secretary's house or under the stage of a social club. Proof of this neglect is the survival of *just* twenty-three banners from over 200 pits in the Northumberland coalfield. Of course not every colliery had a banner, but old photographs of the Annual Northumberland Miners' Picnic offer tantalizing glimpses of lost banners. Where are the banners from Choppington 'A' pit and the collieries of Horton Grange and Netherton? What has become of the fine Tutill damask silk banner which represented the pitmen of North Seaton Colliery until 1959, or the old banner paraded by the Dudley miners before it was discarded in favour of a more up-to-date one?

Over the past decade miners' banners, instead of proclaiming a confident pride in their union and industry, have been silent witnesses at the key events in the rapid erosion of the coal industry. It was the lodge banners which led the miners' poignant return to work in 1985 at the end of their year-long strike. The frenzy of rallies and demonstrations against the pit closures' announcement of October 1992 saw banners once again being carried through the streets of London. Yet unemployment, part-time and casual work, the demise of heavy industry and anti-union legislation continue to contribute to the decline in union membership. As a result, few new banners are being commissioned and opportunities to fly banners are rare. The miners, chief among the banner bearers, are not the force they used to be, particularly since the mass closure and privatization programme of the 1990s. So what of the future?

Despite the casual approach to preserving union history, a huge number of 'homeless' banners are now emerging as union membership declines, branches close and unions amalgamate. Rather late in the day, historians, museum curators and trade unionists are recognizing the extent of their task in protecting these banners from decay and oblivion. Banners will never be paraded through the streets of Britain in the vast numbers of their heyday in the 1880s and 1890s. With imagination and perseverance, however, homes can be found for them in museums and other local institutions such as churches, town halls, libraries, schools and welfare institutes. The future of banners such as those in the Northumberland collection must be assured because they are unique testaments to the struggles and achievements of the trade union movement, and their messages of unity and comradeship are as relevant today as they were when first unfurled.

7 Miners' banners of Northumberland: *an illustrated catalogue*

ASHINGTON GROUP OF COLLIERIES (PLATES 1 & 2)

This is probably the oldest surviving Northumberland miners' banner and, with its woven silk damask border and skilfully painted central medallions, it is an example of George Tutill's workmanship at its best. Both sides are standard Tutill designs, frequently selected by lodges from his catalogue. It is very much a banner of its time. The confident slogans, the imagery and costume suggest the early 1920s and the Ashington Mineworkers' Federation minutes verify this, with entries recording the banner's presence at the 1925 Annual Miners' Picnic and at rallies during the 1926 strike.

Coal mining began in the Ashington area in 1854 with the sinking of the Fell-'em-Doon Pit. Further shafts were sunk and collectively they came to be known as the Ashington Colliery. This colliery, along with four others – Woodhorn, Linton, Ellington and Lynemouth – formed the powerful Ashington Coal Company, and the Ashington Mineworkers' Federation represented the miners employed at these pits. Although by the 1930s the Federation was mainly concerned with welfare issues, in the 1920s it played a pivotal role in local industrial relations directing, for example, the action of the Ashington miners during the 1926 General Strike.

The years immediately following the First World War (1914–18) were characterized by industrial unrest in Britain. The miners were at the forefront of this activity and their banners often reflected their political aspirations. The 'vision' of a better life, as depicted on the front, is a recurring theme on banners of this period. Indeed versions of this very design appear on many Durham miners' banners and several National Union of Railwaymen banners now held at the National Museum of Labour History in Manchester. The romantic symbolism of the maypole and female figure in classical dress is borrowed from the 1894 cartoon, 'The Workers' Maypole', by the socialist artist, Walter Crane. The exhortation, 'workers of the world unite', and the ideal of the 'co-operative commonwealth' reflect the socialist convictions for a planned, rational society held by many union leaders of the time. The banner also suggests a Syndicalist influence. Syndicalism was at its height before the First World War; its advocates believed that society was dependent on industrial workers and that the only way that they could exert power was by joining together in large industrial unions. The group of workers gathered round the crate possibly represents the Triple Alliance which was formed in 1915 and comprised the miners, transport workers and railway men. The reverse of the banner is no less polemical; it presents a powerful case for the nationalization of the coal industry.

Since the late nineteenth century, the miners had been campaigning for the nationalization of the coal industry. In 1917 the Prime Minister, Lloyd George, announced the state control of the pits but only as an emergency wartime measure. After the war, in 1919, the Government set up a Committee of Inquiry into the coal industry known as the Sankey Commission, after its chairman Justice Sankey. The commission voted in favour of nationalization but, to the great disappointment of the miners, Lloyd George rejected this recommendation. The 'Plea for Nationalization' on the Ashington banner is illustrated by a George-and-the-Dragon image. An heroic male figure rises out of a fiery pit-head to slay the dragon of 'profit and private ownership' with a spear bearing the words 'state control'.

Beneath is a scene very evocative of the First World War. It portrays a funeral procession with the coffin borne on the shoulders of the mourners, followed by rows of men sporting the flat caps and moustaches so typical of the period. In the front row are the walking wounded with eye patch, arm sling and crutches. The message is clear: as long as the coal industry remains in private hands, the toll on the workforce will remain high. With Lloyd George's rejection of the Sankey Commission's recommendation to nationalize the pits, the banner's message was to prove topical for over a quarter of a century.

ASHINGTON MINEWORKERS' FEDERATION (PLATES 3, 4 & 5)

'A letter from the Ashington miners was read asking that the Federation discuss the question of purchasing a new banner. After discussion it was agreed that the Secretary make enquiries regarding prices etc.' So ran the minutes of the Federation committee meeting held on Sunday 27 February 1949. The Ashington miners 'Plea for Nationalization', so emotively expressed on their old banner, was at last granted in 1947 by the post-war Labour government. In response the Ashington Federation, like union lodges across the nation's coalfields, commissioned a new banner to celebrate this victory.

Unfortunately this banner is not 'signed' by its maker, but the fine scroll work and high quality illustrations suggest Tutill's workmanship. As with many banners, it is difficult to discern which is the front and which the back; however when the banner is flown the side depicting the five Ashington pits is usually to the fore. Mineworkers take great pride in their industry and many colliery banners carry images of miners hewing coal, their tools and machinery and detailed colliery scenes. The Ashington Federation banner is typical of this genre and the five pit scenes are very accurate.

The reverse of the banner is a tribute to nationalization. It carries a romantic scene of a miner, his wife, small son and daughter standing against the backdrop of a colliery; their arms are raised, welcoming the dawn of nationalization. The miner wears his pit clothes and carries a compressed air drill. There are actually three surviving Ashington Federation banners and they all bear the same illustrations, but with one striking difference which provides the clue to their respective dates. The earliest banner, made in 1949 and mentioned in the Federation minute-book, portrays the miner's wife in the modest costume of the post-war austerity years. On the second banner she sports the white stiletto heels and full skirts of the 1950s. The third banner, made in 1984, hangs in the council chamber of Wansbeck District Council in Ashington. It was made by the Nuneaton banner-making company of Toye, Kenning and Spencer and was a faithful copy of the 1950s version.

The Federation banner was carried at the annual Miners' Picnic by banner men drawn from all the member collieries. In later years, several of these collieries acquired their own banners and the Federation banner was flown by the Ashington lodge until the pit's closure in 1988.

BOMARSUND (PLATES 6 & 7)

The Bomarsund banner is another fine example of George Tutill's craftsmanship. It was made at the company's Chesham premises in Buckinghamshire as the signature on the front of the banner clearly states. Its unusual design, however, was the work of a local man, Mr Don Sutherland, who at the time was a chief engineer for the NCB. The banner firmly belongs to the post-nationalization period and, as the date on the reverse indicates, it was made in 1953. This is corroborated by a barometer (now in the possession of his family) which was presented to Mr Sutherland in June 1953 in recognition of his work on the design. The skilfully executed pictures on the front of the banner celebrate a double victory, that of nationalization in 1947 and Bomarsund in 1854. The Bomarsund Colliery was named after the Russian fortress captured by the British naval force during the Crimean War. News of this significant capture reached Northumberland just as the Barrington Coal Company was laying the foundations of a row of cottages which were to house the men employed to sink the new shaft. To commemorate this naval victory, the sinkers' row was called Bomarsund.

The reverse of the banner draws a question mark over future sources of power and presents its audience with a stark choice between coal or nuclear power. Set against the backdrop of a globe, perhaps suggesting the global impact of this debate, are two medallions. The first one is a green suburban scene of semi-detached housing with an impressive outcrop of coal on the horizon; next to it is a scene of nuclear devastation. The motive behind the lodge's decision to commission this unusual design is unknown, but it is possible that the miners of Bomarsund felt rather uncertain about the future of their pit with the new technology of nuclear power threatening the market for coal. Today, over forty years later, the banner's message still has resonance.

BRENKLEY AND SEATON BURN (PLATE 8)

The design of this banner is the least elaborate in the Northumberland collection and its functional appearance probably reflects the circumstances under which it was made. As former branch member, George Graham, recalls, during the 1984–5 miners' strike the branch committee decided that they needed a banner and commissioned the North Shields sail-makers, Thomas Young and Son Limited, to make one. The result is a neatly finished, if rather uninspired banner. The yellow silk lettering and pick motifs which appear on both sides of the banner are appliquéed on to blue silk-like material. 'Retain the old unity' proclaims the front of the banner, celebrating the unity which existed between the men of the Brenkley Drift and their colleagues at the nearby Seaton Burn Colliery which closed in 1963. In December 1985, just nine months after the end of the year-long miners' strike, the Brenkley Drift also closed.

BURRADON AND WEETSLADE (PLATE 9)

The Burradon and Weetslade banner is a standard post-nationalization design popular amongst NUM branches across the country. It is clearly the work of an experienced banner-maker, possibly Tutill. The stepped motif on the obverse of the banner is a recurrent image on colliery banners of the post-war period, unashamedly copied by less able banner-makers (for example the Doctor Pit banner). It shows a miner climbing the steps towards socialism, each step marking a goal of the Labour Government of 1945. In the top left- and right-hand corners are small medallions bearing portraits of two popular Labour leaders, Keir Hardie (1856–1916) and Clement Attlee (1883–1967).

As a Scottish miner and the creator of the Independent Labour Party (ILP), Hardie appeared on more miners' banners than any other leader. In 1892, after a trade-union career which combined journalism and the organization of the Scottish miners, Hardie entered Parliament as MP for South West Ham in London. With an interruption of five years, Hardie was an MP until his death in 1916. He doggedly championed the working-class cause and in 1906 became the first leader of the Parliamentary Labour Party. (For a longer biography, see the West Sleekburn banner [25].)

As the leader of the first majority Labour Government, Attlee was in many ways the true inheritor of Hardie's legacy. Yet he was an unlikely hero of the miners, with his middle-class background (he was the son of a solicitor) and Oxford education. As a result of his experience working and living in the East End of London, Attlee joined the ILP and in 1922 was elected to Parliament. In 1935 he was elected leader of the Labour Party and, although his election appeared at the time to be an interim measure, he remained leader until 1955. Attlee led the Labour Party in the wartime coalition government serving in the War Cabinet. It was not, however, until the Labour landslide victory in the 1945 General Election and the rapid introduction of legislation such as the National Health Service and the nationalization of the coal industry that Attlee became a hero of the miners and a popular speaker at the Northumberland Miners' Picnic.

'Education and advancement' is the subject of the reverse of the Burradon banner, and the imposing façade, although not based on a local building, probably represents a training college. The miners appreciated the power of an educated workforce and education is a familiar theme on their banners. Indeed, the same college-like building appears on miners' banners from North Gawber and Kellingley in Yorkshire.

The banner carries the names of two pits, Burradon and Weetslade, which were both owned by the Hazlerigg and Burradon Coal Company at the time of nationalization in 1947. Weetslade Colliery had a relatively short life, producing coal between 1901 and 1966, whilst Burradon drew coals from 1820 through to 1975. The exact date of this banner's manufacture is unknown, but as it bears Attlee's portrait it is likely to have been made between 1947 and 1951, after nationalization and before the defeat of the Labour Government. At some point in its history the banner was badly damaged and, sadly, a decision was made – perhaps by a well-meaning branch official – to 'tidy it up' by removing the lower edge. After the closure of Burradon pit the banner was hung in the miners' village hut, where it remained until 1983 when a former lodge official suggested it be moved to the local school.

CAMBOIS AND BATES (PLATE 10)

This banner was possibly made by the Tutill company for the NUM branch at Cambois Colliery. The colliery was opened around 1862 in the small seaport village called Cambois, pronounced locally as 'cammus'. The banner's striking design represents a significant departure from the traditional heroic miners and socialist utopias framed in elaborate scroll work. The Cambois lodge committee rejected the naturalistic figure paintings, so popular with Tutill and his contemporaries, in favour of a more abstract design whose impact relies more on colour, symbol and bold lettering. Made in 1950, it is another tribute to nationalization and the reverse of the banner depicts a rising sun, a common symbol on post-1947 banners, with the letters of nationalization painted between the rays. Below is a rather gloomy pit scene, overshadowed by a spoil heap.

In contrast are the pit buildings on the front of the banner; they are painted in much warmer tones with the NCB sign clearly visible. Above is a safety lamp, encircled in rings of yellow and gold. The miner's lamp is a very evocative symbol for the mining industry and, with its strong association with safety, it was frequently employed by the NUM. Both sides of the banner carry the branch name skilfully signwritten onto flowing scrolls. The original banner, as early 1950s' photographs of the Annual Miners' Picnic show, was commissioned by the Cambois Colliery branch but sometime in the late 1950s or 1960s the word 'branch' was overpainted with the name of the Blyth pit of Bates. Cambois Colliery closed in 1968 and many men were transferred to Bates and Mill collieries, also in Blyth.

DOCTOR PIT (PLATE 11)

Doctor Pit in Bedlington was so called because one of the Bedlington Coal Company's directors, Dr John Moore Bates of Newcastle, cut the first sod when the pit was sunk in 1852. The colliery closed over a century later, in 1968. Unfortunately the date the banner was made is unknown but it is clearly from the post-war period, bearing a poorer version of the popular stepped motif, showing the gradual progress towards socialism. The front carries an idealized mining family welcoming an angel wearing a Labour Party sash. The figures are rather wooden and the overall effect suggests a naïve style of painting which is not without its own charm.

Sadly, all records about the manufacture of this banner have been lost; however, it is possibly the work of more than one craftsman. In contrast to the naïve appearance of the main images, the quality of the four portraits suggests the hand of a more skilled artist. The two medallions on the front of the banner bear portraits of Robert Smillie, on the left, and Thomas Burt, on the right. The back carries portraits of the two younger figures of A.J. Cook, on the left, and Emmanuel Shinwell, on the right.

The decision by the miners of Doctor Pit to portray Thomas Burt (1837–1922) on their banner is surprising. Despite the vital role he played in shaping the history of the Northumberland miners' union, his contribution is rarely celebrated through banner portraiture. Throughout his life Burt remained faithful to his liberal principles and to the Liberal Party, and his neglect by the pit lodges of Northumberland is probably because of his rejection of the newly formed Labour Party at the end of the nineteenth century. He was born in Northumberland and at the age of ten joined his father in the mines. He soon became involved in trade unionism and in 1865 he was elected agent and secretary of the new Northumberland Miners' Association. He held these two offices until 1905, when he resigned as secretary, but he continued as agent until his retirement in 1913. This long service is all the more remarkable because from 1874 to 1918 Burt was also MP for Morpeth.

Robert Smillie (1857–1940), a more popular figure on miners' banners than Burt, also represented the constituents of Morpeth but as a Labour MP from 1923 to 1929. Like his close friend, Keir Hardie, Smillie had a Scottish mining background and was a founding member of the ILP. In 1894 he was elected president of the Scottish Miners' Federation and in 1912 he took on the presidency of the Miners' Federation of Great Britain (MFGB). As the president he skilfully presented the miners' case at the Sankey Commission of 1919 which recommended nationalization of the coal industry.

Arthur James Cook (1885–1931) was born in Somerset in 1883 and stands with Keir Hardie as one of the miners' most admired leaders. Cook rejected his father's occupation as a regular soldier and became a farm labourer. At the age of sixteen he left the land to work in the mines of the Rhondda Valley in South Wales and this marked the beginning of his career as an active trade unionist. In 1919 he was elected a union agent in the Rhondda and only five years later he became general secretary of the MFGB. He was a true agitator and the General Strike of 1926 was his finest hour. He regularly spoke in the coalfields of Northumberland and Durham and his fiery oratory inspired great devotion amongst the miners, even though his Labour contemporaries were very wary of his militant rhetoric. Cook never really recovered from the bitter defeat of the miners when they were ordered to return to work at the end of 1926, and he died of cancer five years later.

'Manny' Shinwell MP (1884–1986), in contrast to Cook, lived to be 102 and his politics mellowed with age, enabling him to adopt a back-bench 'elder statesman' role. Yet back in Glasgow in 1921 his militancy earned him a five months' prison sentence for incitement to riot. In 1935 he was elected MP for the Durham mining constituency of Seaham Harbour, ousting Ramsay MacDonald who was regarded by many as a traitor to the Labour Party because of his willingness to lead the National Government of 1931. Shinwell's popularity really soared amongst the miners when, as Minister of Fuel and Power, he oversaw the nationalization of the coal industry in 1947.

DUDLEY (PLATE 12)

The Dudley banner is a product of the Tutill studio in Chesham, Buckinghamshire but is not an inspiring example of the company's craftsmanship. It has a very simple, functional design. The usual ornate scroll work frames large central medallions on both front and back; however, they contain not pictures but slogans. 'Strength through unity' is blazoned on the front whilst the message continues vertically on the back with: '**C**onveys **O**ur **A**ims **L**iterally.' This acrostic, possibly composed by the branch committee, was obviously chosen because the first letters of each word spell 'coal'. The modest nature of this banner suggests that the branch had limited funds to spend.

The precise date of this banner's manufacture is unknown, but it was likely to have been made in the 1960s or early 1970s. In fact the reverse of the banner carries the number '561' which may refer to the date of manufacture, that is, May 1961. Photographic evidence from the 1950s reveals that the Dudley lodge had an earlier banner which sported two large portraits. A reference is also made, presumably to this earlier banner, in the Seghill NUM branch minute-book recording the receipt of an invitation from the Dudley lodge to the banner's unfurling ceremony in 1948. Unfortunately nothing more is known about this banner's appearance or its whereabouts. The older generation of banners, once they had been made redundant by the commissioning of a new one, were usually destroyed, lost or left to moulder in a damp cellar or attic. The Tutill banner represented the Dudley miners until their pit closed in 1977 but, in contrast to its predecessor, it was saved by its community and now hangs in a local primary school.

ELLINGTON (PLATES 13 & 14)

This banner has a special place in local people's affections as its design is the work of the pitman painter, Oliver Kilbourn (1904–93). He was the most prominent member of the Ashington Group, members (mostly miners) of a Workers' Educational Association class who began to paint together in 1934.

Having studied evolution, the class decided to try art history. In order to encourage an understanding of the principles of art appreciation, the class tutor took an innovative step and invited his students to experiment with brush, palette and paint. By 1936 the class had evolved into the Ashington Group and was exhibiting work in Newcastle. The paintings, many of which survive today and hang in Woodhorn Colliery Museum, vividly portray life and work in Ashington. The Group members continued to meet and paint long after the classes ceased and for Oliver Kilbourn, a working miner for more than fifty years, art became a passionate interest which he pursued between shifts at the pit and into retirement.

By the early 1950s the Group was a well-established part of Ashington life and it seemed fitting that when the Ellington NUM branch decided in 1950 to commission a banner, they should turn to the Ellington miner and painter, Oliver Kilbourn. Kilbourn's banner, unlike the standard Tutill catalogue designs, offers a more personal tribute to nationalization. 'Nationalization was a realization of the miners' dreams,' recalls Kilbourn's widow, and, 'Oliver's banner was inspired by this.' He chose to represent the post-war era through housing.

The front of the banner carries a grim scene of colliery terraces set against dark pit heaps and smoking chimneys. 'Close the door on past dreariness' runs the slogan, also created by Oliver Kilbourn, and continues on the other side with, 'Open it to future brightness'. These words are illustrated by a light and airy vision of semi-detached houses with trees and neat gardens. The red tiled roofs and Tudor-style beams suggest a 1930s' Garden City suburbia, a popular motif on union banners evoking a rural utopian future. The old colliery rows depicted on the front reveal more about Kilbourn as an artist and the way he brought personal experience to his art. A professional artist working in a distant studio would never have included details such as the fly posters on the left-hand gable-end, the washing strung across the street or the row of 'netties' (toilets) running down the centre. Another testament to Kilbourn's mining background are the doors framing the two scenes, as they represent the trap doors which controlled the circulation of air in the pit.

According to the Ellington lodge minute-book for 1951, Oliver Kilbourn presented several designs to the committee and they selected the most appropriate. Kilbourn was then left to liaise with a sadly unnamed firm of banner-makers over the translation of his watercolour designs on to the painted silk banner. The end result was flown for the first time at the 1951 Annual Miners' Picnic in Morpeth. Further entries in the minute-book reveal that the purchase of the banner was a significant financial burden for the branch; funds were raised through a Christmas draw, dances and a levy of all branch members. It proved, however, to be a sound investment for the banner served the lodge for just over thirty years. In 1982, following three years of running repairs after each Picnic, the branch commissioned a new banner. Much to Oliver Kilbourn's surprise, the new banner, made by the professional banner-makers of Toye, Kenning and Spencer Limited, was a faithful copy of the 1950s' design. This banner still represents the miners of Ellington. Ellington, which is owned by R.J. Budge Mining Limited, is the only deep mine left in the North East.

LYNEMOUTH (PLATE 15)

This banner is perhaps the most unusual in the Northumberland collection and indeed its idiosyncratic design is possibly unique amongst miners' banners nationally. The letters NUM emblazoned on the front and the idyllic rural scene of a boy and girl in 1940s' dress 'Looking for the Sunrise' of socialism suggest that it is a post-nationalization banner and this is confirmed by oral testimony. The banner was acquired for the Newbiggin branch of the NUM in the early 1950s and the branch treasurer, Charles Carr, was responsible for its design. His daughter, Jean Mackay, recalls that a child's drawing found in her father's garden provided the inspiration for the image on the front of the banner (they lived close to a local school). The reverse of the banner carries a picture of Christ standing by a globe and Jean Mackay believes this unusual image reflected her father's strong faith. Unfortunately nothing is known about the banner maker who transferred Charles Carr's design on to fabric. The painting style is naïve and the lettering, although proficient, displays none of the showmanship of the professionally made banners usually favoured by pit branch officials. Unusually, the images and slogans have been painted on to two lengths of woven wool rather than the traditional silk. The rectangular shape, the absence of elaborate scroll work, the red and yellow colour scheme, plus the style of the lettering, are all reminiscent of local Labour Party banners of the period. This influence is quite possible as links between local Labour Parties and pit lodges were always very strong.

The slogan on the front of the banner is unusually striking because of its length and its didactic tone. The future will be yours, it confidently proclaims to NUM members, if you ensure that your union is well organized and your members well educated. This will be achieved by promoting the benefits of trade unionism ('spread the light') and ensuring solidarity by increasing the membership ('look to the register'). This political message is in stark contrast to the Christian sentiment on the reverse of the banner. A Christ-like figure stands over a globe accompanied by the quotation, 'My Peace I leave with you.'

This banner was originally made for the Newbiggin Colliery and local people can remember the banner being blessed at St Bartholomew's Church before branch officials paraded it through the streets. In 1967, when the pit at Newbiggin closed, the men and their banner were transferred to Lynemouth and the old branch name was overpainted. The decision to hand over the banner was probably made by the branch officials and was not popular amongst the old miners, who would have preferred to have held on to it as a memorial to Newbiggin's mining past which spanned fifty-nine years. Since 1980, when coal production ceased at Lynemouth Colliery, the banner has represented the men who work at the Lynemouth coal preparation plant which washes coals drawn from nearby Ellington Colliery and open cast coal sites. When the banner is not being flown, it is usually on display at the Lynemouth Welfare Institute.

MILL, ISABELLA, BATES (PLATE 16)

This banner was last flown in 1986 when Bates Colliery closed after a long and bitter battle to save Blyth's last pit. Another example of a post-1947 banner, it symbolizes the confidence and pride that nationalization gave the miners in their industry and celebrates the unity of Blyth miners from the three pits of Mill, Isabella and Bates.

Coal mining contributed much to the prosperity of the Northumberland port of Blyth and was a key employer for local people. Nearly two hundred years ago, two pits were sunk at Cowpen, two miles east of Blyth. They were known as North Pit (1799–1896) and South Pit (1695–1911), and they were joined by Isabella in 1849 and Crofton Mill Colliery in 1886, better known as Mill. In 1928 a new pit called Bates was sunk. Isabella closed in 1966 and Mill three years later. Most of the pitmen were transferred to Bates, which was being developed into a showpiece pit by the NCB.

The exact date of this banner's manufacture is unknown, but it is likely to have been sometime in the 1950s when the three Blyth pits of Mill, Isabella and Bates were in full production. The front of the banner bears the name of Cowpen and Crofton NUM branch and the names of the three member pits. Below is a collection of images celebrating the coal industry: two miners toil underground and above them stands a plinth supporting a modernized NCB pit and the immortal word 'industry'. References to the port of Blyth can be seen in the seascape and the coat of arms. The theme of modernization is carried onto the reverse of the banner with a scene of a modern pit, possibly Bates, complete with an 'A' frame headstock. After the closure of Mill and Isabella, the miners of Bates flew this banner as their own.

NORTH SEATON (PLATE 17)

This banner was probably made in 1959, the year North Seaton Colliery celebrated its centenary and only two years before it closed in 1961. Photographic evidence from the 1955 and 1956 Miners' Picnics reveals that this rather subdued banner replaced a more traditional one, which bore elaborate scroll work, a female figure draped in classical dress holding a chalice and the legend 'Labour Government 1945. Peace and Plenty. The hope of the world'. Sadly this banner has since been lost or destroyed, and its replacement carries a more conservative message. The front bears the ever-popular trade union slogan 'Unity is Strength', and a rather surprising Union Jack, and the back depicts a miner in the blue overalls of the 1950s marching towards 'Progress' accompanied by the words: 'Always Forward'.

Although the banner is competently made by a London firm known simply as C.A.S. Limited, it is rather disappointing. It lacks the inspiring message of its predecessor and even its colouring is restrained. The traditional scarlet, royal blue, gold and silver are absent and instead the words and images are painted onto an improbable peach-coloured rayon silk. Yet, despite its rather inauspicious appearance, it has had a short but interesting history. In 1959 two men were killed at North Seaton Colliery and people can recall the banner being draped in black ribbons at the Miners' Picnic to mark these fatalities. When the colliery closed the banner went missing for several years. It was finally discovered in 1991, in pristine condition, under the stage of the North Seaton Miners' Welfare Institute. The Institute has since been pulled down but the banner is preserved at Woodhorn Colliery Museum.

NORTH WALBOTTLE (PLATES 18 &19)

This is the finest banner in the Woodhorn collection and first impressions suggest that it is also the oldest surviving Northumberland banner. As the signature woven into the lower edge of the banner indicates, it was made by George Tutill when his company was still based at 83 City Road, London. Like many of the older Tutill banners produced at the London premises, it is made of one piece of damask woven silk. Unfortunately, the Jacquard loom on which these damask squares were woven was not reassembled when the Tutill company moved to Chesham in Buckinghamshire, after suffering bomb damage in 1940 during the Blitz.

Coal production at North Walbottle began in 1892 and the symbols and allegorical figures which crowd the front of the banner are very typical of nineteenth-century banners. In fact, according to an illustration in the 1885 Tutill catalogue, exactly the same design served as the Arms of the Order of the Norfolk and Norwich Unity of Oddfellows. Yet all this evidence pointing to a late nineteenth-century date of manufacture is contradicted by the words 'National Union of Mineworkers' emblazoned on both sides of the banner. (The Miners' Federation of Great Britain became the NUM in January 1945 to coincide with nationalization two years later.) Of course the banner could have been overpainted with the new name of the union, but no evidence of this was found by the textile conservator who worked on the banner. In the absence of documentary evidence to clarify this apparent anomaly, the history of the banner can only be surmised. It is known that a number of damask woven squares survived the bombing of Tutill's London premises in 1940. It is possible that the North Walbottle branch was offered one of these squares painted up with a design selected from the Tutill catalogue by the branch officials. The exact date of this banner will probably remain a mystery; the origin and significance of the vivid imagery on the front of the banner, however, can be explained.

The architectural plinth which provides a pedestal for the figures and symbols gives the banner a sombre respectability. This classically inspired backdrop was shared by trade-union emblems or certificates also produced by the entrepreneurial Mr Tutill and so popular amongst trade unionists at the end of the nineteenth century. The North Walbottle banner bears two female allegorical figures also derived from classical imagery. On the left is Justice, wearing a crown and holding a sword which signify her power; the scales of impartiality are depicted on the globe behind her. The significance of the figure on the right is less clear; her victorious laurel crown combined with the globe may mean she represents Truth. Alternatively the torch or caduceus which she holds could signify Mercury, the messenger. Between these female figures is the popular Christian image of a proud lion lying next to the gentle lamb. An elaborate horn of plenty overflowing with flowers and fruit is also depicted, conveying a sense of rejoicing and abundance. The presence of the sun, moon and stars suggests either a biblical reference to the fourth day of creation or the opposites of night and day. Another set of opposites is suggested by the celestial globe on the left and the terrestrial globe on the right. Beneath these figures and symbols fly two baroque-like angels or cherubs; the one on the right is gazing into a mirror which often symbolizes truth and perhaps echoes the female allegorical figure above. These two winged infants support a shield which carries yet more symbols. Noah's ark is depicted, representing the church and protection, and above it flies the dove, an emblem of good tidings and peace. The hourglass is an attribute of Father Time and death, whilst the skull and crossbones also symbolize death. In contrast, the hand with a heart in its palm symbolizes friendship and faithfulness.

This eclectic collection of figures and symbols owes more to its origin as a Friendly Society banner than its adoption as a union banner. There are, however, two images, the clasped hands and the all-seeing eye, which recur in trade-union iconography. The all-seeing eye was a device adapted by Friendly Societies from eighteenth-century Freemasonry imagery. The Freemasons, in turn, borrowed this all-seeing eye of the Almighty from craft guilds. The Friendly Societies and trade unions of the nineteenth century, as they attempted to consolidate their memberships, protect funds and curb the independent action of members, gave the all-seeing eye a more prosaic role. For them, it was the eye of the central executive or the general secretary! The clasped hands, which occur in miniature on the front of the banner, dominate the reverse, amplifying the accompanying slogan of 'Unity is strength'. The backdrop of a globe adds an international angle to this message. This fine banner was taken out of action in 1968 when North Walbottle Colliery closed.

PEGSWOOD (PLATES 20 & 21)

This striking banner is very evocative of the post-war period. The reverse carries portraits of five miners' heroes whilst the front takes nationalization as its theme, offering an alternative to the traditional depictions of mechanization and welfare as symbols of nationalization. Instead it celebrates Vesting Day, 1 January 1947, when the coal industry was finally nationalized. It was a triumphant day for the miners and the Pegswood banner captures the sense of occasion. A group of men and women, in oddly old-fashioned clothing for 1947, stand at the pit head looking up at the sign, which was erected at every colliery. It bears the immortal words: 'This colliery is managed by the NCB on behalf of the people'. Above the crowd flutters the familiar blue NCB flag.

As the picture on the front of the banner suggests, the banner was probably made in 1947 or 1948. Although the Pegswood NUM minute-book for this period has been lost, this date is corroborated by an entry in the Ashington Federation minutes in March 1949 recording an inquiry made by the Secretary of the Federation about the recently purchased Pegswood banner. The probable maker of the banner is revealed in the Pegswood minutes for 1952, when the branch committee discussed the deterioration of the banner and requested the Secretary to ask the Birmingham regalia company of Fattorini about reconditioning. The banner's condition must have been stabilized as there are few references to it over the ensuing three years. In 1955, however, the branch commissioned a new banner which probably served the miners of Pegswood until 1969 when their pit closed, just three years short of its centenary. (The later banner was handed over to the Whittle lodge and is discussed below.)

The back of the banner carries five fine portraits of miners' leaders who 'blazed the trail' to the Labour victory of 1945 and nationalization. The two remarkable Scottish mining trade unionists, Keir Hardie and Robert Smillie, who were also key founders of the Independent Labour Party, are portrayed alongside the hero of the 1926 General Strike, A.J. Cook, and the architect of nationalization, Manny Shinwell, Minister of Fuel and Power in 1947. (These four leaders are discussed above under the Doctor Pit and Burradon banners.) The central portrait is of the Northumberland miners' leader, William Straker (1855–1941). The son of an agricultural labourer, he was born and brought up in rural Northumberland. After working as a farm boy, Straker entered the mines at the age of seventeen. In 1879 he was elected delegate for the Widdrington lodge and over the following three decades he gradually rose through the ranks of the Northumberland miners' union taking over the general secretaryship from Thomas Burt in 1913.

RISING SUN, WALLSEND (PLATE 22)

The Rising Sun Colliery was named after the nearby Rising Sun Farm. It was established in 1906 by the Wallsend and Hebburn Coal Company and coals were first drawn two years later. During the 1950s the colliery was substantially modernized by the NCB and the front of the banner commemorates this with a picture of the third shaft sunk in 1955. For the miners, nationalization meant a considerable investment by the NCB in their safety, and the modernization and mechanization of their work environment, and these three issues are celebrated on the Rising Sun banner. Yet, despite these advances, nationalization also heralded an extensive programme of pit closures in the 1950s and 1960s and the reverse of the banner stresses the unity of the men at the Rising Sun Pit who were drawn from eight former collieries across the Northumberland coalfield. They were the four Throckley pits of Blutcher, Coronation, Isabella and Maria which closed in the early to mid-1950s, plus Seghill, Mickley, West Wylam and Montague, all of which closed in the late 1950s and early 1960s.

The banner is signed 'Tutill, Chesham' and its design demonstrates how the Tutill company's artistry began to decline in the post-war period. Whilst the sign-writing displays the usual flair and competency of the Tutill studios, the pit scene is rather bleak, lacking the detail of earlier colliery pictures, and the rising sun image on the back is unusually simplistic. The banner was possibly made in 1962 to coincide with the closure of Seghill, the last of the collieries listed on the reverse to shut. Sadly, the banner's appearances at Picnics were limited because the Rising Sun Pit also became a victim of the NCB's drive to rationalize and it was closed in 1969.

SEGHILL (PLATE 23)

The Seghill banner is rather unusual; it is shield-shaped and, instead of the traditional silk, it is made of woven wool fabric. Both sides of the banner have applied panels of painted wool fabric whilst some of the lettering has been painted directly onto the fabric. The style is naïve and it is easy to understand why it has this 'home made' quality when one reads the account of its manufacture in the Seghill Colliery Branch minute-books.

At a committee meeting held on 2 February 1947, just one month after the coal industry had been nationalized, the branch secretary was asked to write to the firm of 'Tootals' (Tutill) to inquire about a banner. The committee also instructed the secretary to find out the requirement for ration coupons, an important consideration as rationing continued into peacetime. The branch funds probably could not run to a professionally made Tutill banner as there is no further reference to this illustrious banner-maker in the minute-book. Instead, the branch officials consulted a member of the National Coal Board's publicity department, who sent them several designs from which they selected the banner emblems.

The medallion on the front of the banner bears a picture of a colliery with the Houses of Parliament floating above, representing the miners' political ambitions which became a reality in 1945 with the election of the first majority Labour Government. The reverse carries a picture of a miner working at the coal face beside a longwall coal cutter. There is also a smaller image of a village, possibly Seghill, and the slogan 'The will to work is the way to prosperity'. Unfortunately, the branch secretary did not name the banner-maker in the minutes but he did make detailed entries about the unfurling ceremony which the branch officials combined with a presentation of kettles to the residents of the local Aged Miners' Homes! On Sunday 28 September 1947 the Seghill miners paraded their new banner at the Miners' Picnic, but exactly how long this unusual banner represented them is uncertain. A photograph taken in 1961, just one year before the pit's closure, shows the Seghill NUM officials standing with a traditional silk banner; the whereabouts of this banner is unknown.

SLEEKBURN 'A' (PLATE 24)

This striking banner was commissioned by the miners of Bedlington 'A' Pit. The colliery, also known as Sleekburn 'A', was originally called the 'Auld Pit' when sinking began in 1838 under the direction of the Bedlington Coal Company. A fascinating account of the commissioning of this banner is recorded in the minute-book of the Bedlington 'A' Colliery Combined Levy Fund Committee. A resolution to procure a banner which would represent all grades of workmen was carried at the Annual General Meeting of 18 September 1949. The committee men then invited Mr Don Sutherland, 'a chap from Broomhill [who] was fairly skilful as a designer', to come up with a design and they asked the George Tutill banner manufacturers to submit an estimate for the work. A telegram, confirming the commission, was duly sent to the Tutill company in December 1949 and six months later the finished banner was dispatched to the branch, just in time for the Annual Miners' Picnic.

The partnership between Mr Sutherland (he also designed the Bomarsund banner) and George Tutill Limited produced an unusual banner, whose design eschews the ornamental scroll and foliage work usually associated with a Tutill banner. Instead, the illustrations on both sides are framed by a solid gold border. The front of the banner portrays the Houses of Parliament, a recurring image on miners' banners, reflecting their belief that real power lies in Parliament through the election of miners' MPs (for further examples, see Seghill, Burradon and Woodhorn banners). The reverse of the banner celebrates nationalization portraying the benefits of 'the new era' as 'welfare', 'education' and 'mechanization'. Welfare is illustrated with the familiar white pit head baths' building, education is represented by a red brick training college, while a diesel locomotive pulling coal symbolizes mechanization.

The banner's arrival sparked a bustle of activity. It was officially unveiled by the committee's secretary and eighteen pitmen responded to the request for six banner carriers to attend the Miners' Picnic. The committee also made sure that it was insured and they found a permanent home for it at the Bedlington Station Social Club. After its first outing at the Picnic, the committee men carefully unfurled the banner to see how it had fared. Relieved to discover that, barring a small crease in the centre, all was in order they vowed to unroll it every eight weeks! Although it is doubtful that they actually carried out these bimonthly checks, their obvious pride and concern was rewarded. The banner, which probably represented the Sleekburn 'A' miners until the pit's closure in 1971, was in very good condition when it was donated to Woodhorn Colliery Museum nearly forty years after its unfurling.

WEST SLEEKBURN (PLATE 25)

'His vision was our inspiration' proclaims the front of this banner which is dominated by a fine portrait of the miners' most admired Labour leader, James Keir Hardie (1856–1916). Keir Hardie, as he was known, was born in 1856 in a one-roomed cottage at Legbrannock, near Holytown, Lanarkshire. By the age of ten he was working in the pits, but twelve years later union activity cost him his job and he was blacklisted. For the next fourteen years Hardie combined journalism with union activity, organizing the Scottish miners and acting as secretary to the Ayrshire miners' union and the Scottish Miners' Federation. In 1892 he was elected as independent Labour Member of Parliament for South West Ham in London and a year later the ILP was formed with Hardie as chairman. In 1895 he lost his seat, but five years later he was back in Parliament representing Merthyr Burghs. He became known as 'the member for the unemployed' and, wearing his characteristic cloth cap and tweed suit, he championed the socialist cause. Through his oratory, journalism and personal appeal he drew the trade union and labour movement together into an effective alliance. In 1906 he became the first leader of the Parliamentary Labour Party.

Unfortunately this impressive silk banner, probably made in 1950, represented the miners of West Sleekburn for only twelve years. West Sleekburn Colliery, originally called 'The Winning', was sunk in 1859 and was the fourth pit to be added to the Bedlington Coal Company. The colliery, also known as Bedlington 'E' Pit, was taken over by the NCB in 1947. The event is celebrated on the reverse of the banner with the slogan 'Progress by nationalization' and an illustration of the familiar white modernistic buildings which housed the pit-head baths. Ironically, as with so many of the older pits in the Northumberland coalfield, steps towards modernization such as the opening of pit-head baths were closely followed by closure. In 1962 coal production ceased at West Sleekburn Colliery.

Sadly, the maker of the West Sleekburn banner is unknown; however, the high quality of the paintings and sign-writing suggest a professional bannermaker of Tutill's calibre. Interestingly, it shares several design features with the Burradon and Weetslade banner, including a red silk ground with no border and the same portrait of Keir Hardie, with red tie and tweed suit.

WHITTLE (PLATE 26)

This banner originally represented the miners of Pegswood Colliery, near Morpeth. The pit closed in 1969 and several years later, possibly at the time of the miners' strikes of 1972 and 1974, the NUM branch at Whittle adopted it as their own. The Whittle Drift was sunk in 1917 and in 1930 it was taken over by the Co-operative Wholesale Society. Under NCB management Whittle Colliery was substantially modernized in the 1960s, but there is no evidence to suggest that the miners of Whittle were moved to celebrate nationalization and the subsequent modernization of their pit with the purchase of a lodge banner.

The origin of this banner can be traced back to a meeting of the Pegswood NUM branch in early 1955. The committee men, having examined the old banner, decided that its poor state of repair warranted the purchase of a new one. The new banner, designed by a Mr J. Collingwood of Morpeth, probably had its first outing at the 1956 Picnic. The branch officials, however, were not satisfied with it and instructed the Secretary to inquire about ways 'to have the banner brightened up'! The Whittle banner certainly lacks the inspirational quality of earlier banners and its images are painted in a naïve style. The front is rather earnest in tone, proclaiming 'Forward with Socialism' and 'Social and economic security'. It bears portraits, adorned with victorious laurel leaves, of two of Britain's most admired socialists, Keir Hardie (see West Sleekburn for a biography) and Aneurin Bevan, spelt 'Bevin' by the banner artist!

Like Hardie, Bevan (1897–1960) had a mining background and was revered by the miners. He was born in Tredegar, Monmouthshire and followed his father into the pits. It was not long before he was drawn into trade union activity and by 1916 he was chairman of his lodge. During the 1926 General Strike he organized relief for the striking miners but, perhaps because of the failure of the strike, Bevan concluded that change could only be achieved through Parliament and the Labour Party. In 1929 he was elected Labour MP for Ebbw Vale, a seat which he held until his death. Bevan was a brilliant orator and a popular speaker at the Miners' Picnic but his left-wing views made him a controversial member of the Parliamentary Labour Party. On the election of the Labour Government in 1945 he became Minister of Health and Housing and ushered in the National Health Service.

The reverse of the banner carries four painted panels, two of which illustrate the banner's slogan 'Let the lessons of the past serve the future'. The two small oval-shaped emblems portray an old pit scene and the six 'Tolpuddle Martyrs' of 1834. They are being led to the ship which was to carry them to Australia where they had been sentenced to seven years transportation for forming a trade union for agricultural labourers in Dorset. In 1985, at the time of the miners' strike, the two larger panels were repainted by Davison Brennan, a miner who also worked on a number of the Durham banners. One panel depicts a modern pit, the other shows the dead body of William Jobling gibbeted at Jarrow Slake. Jobling was a Jarrow miner who was hanged at Durham for murdering a magistrate during the 1832 miners' strike. Sadly, this banner became redundant soon after its repainting when Whittle Colliery was closed by British Coal in 1987. At the time of writing, Whittle Drift is being worked as a private mine producing high quality coal for the domestic market but with a much reduced and largely non-union workforce.

WOODHORN (PLATE 27)

On Saturday 11 June 1960 six miners from Woodhorn in Ashington carried their colliery's first banner through the streets to the Miners' Picnic. Although coal had been mined at Woodhorn since 1894, until that year the pit lodge does not seem to have had its own banner, preferring to elect two men to help carry the Ashington Federation banner at the Annual Picnic. At a committee meeting in June 1959, however, the branch officials agreed to purchase a banner. They commissioned an unnamed company in Birmingham to make the banner and placed adverts in the local papers inviting people to submit designs, offering a prize of £10. The new banner, designed by Mr W. Jones and Mr J. Riddle, was unfurled on 7 May 1960 at a formal ceremony at Hirst Welfare in Ashington, attended by union officials and the colliery's manager and under-manager. After the ceremony the banner was paraded through the streets led by the colliery band.

Despite the elaborate plans surrounding the banner's design and unfurling, its appearance was a disappointment to the branch members. The original design was dismissed as having a 'Japanese look' and the branch officials were discussing the redesign of the front of the banner as early as November 1960. Its rather primitive painted design portrayed a bare-chested miner standing astride a bridge inscribed with 'Woodhorn Branch'. The bridge spans the gap between two cliffs; on one cliff stands Burt Hall, the Northumberland NUM's headquarters, and the opposite cliff supports a colliery. The backdrop is a sun with very prominent rays, reminiscent of the Japanese rising sun motif. The actual date when this medallion was replaced is unclear but the surviving banner, held by the museum now occupying Woodhorn Colliery, carries the second design.

The origin of the second medallion is a mystery. It may have come from another banner which, judging from its worn appearance, had had a lot of use. Like the original illustration, it is painted in a naïve style. The circular design is divided into several segments portraying the modernization of the coal industry. A modern 'A' frame headstock and underground man rider are depicted opposite dark images of an old pit village and hand hewing at the coal face. The Houses of Parliament are also present plus the slogan: 'A century of coal' and the dates 1925, 1950 and 1975.

The reverse of the banner is, by comparison, very simple. In a style borrowed from the Cambois and Bates banner, the branch name is painted onto two scrolls which are appliquéed onto the banner along with the letters 'NUM'. Beneath is the slogan: 'The miners' shield and armour' which is illustrated by body armour and a shield. Despite resistance over two decades, the NUM was unable to 'shield' its members at Woodhorn from the closure of their pit in 1981.

The 1957 Northumberland Miners' Picnic. For some the speeches and banners made it an important political meeting, for many more it was a family day out.

ACKNOWLEDGEMENTS

I am indebted to the following organizations and people for the support and help they so generously gave me whilst researching and writing this book : Janet Allan, Blyth Valley Borough Council, Burradon Primary School, Philip Dunn, Norman Emery, Fordley Community Primary School, John Gorman, George Graham, William Harris, Margaret Kilbourn, Jean Mackay, George Muirhead, Dennis Murphy, National Coal Mining Museum for England, National Museum of Labour History, National Union of Mineworkers, Northumberland Area, Newcastle Society of Antiquaries, Northumberland County Record Office, Caroline Rendell, George Stephenson, Alan Sutherland, James Tuck, Alec Wallace, Wansbeck District Council, Penny Wilkinson and Woodhorn Colliery Museum.

The illustrations are reproduced courtesy of the following: Stan Gamester, the illustration on page 3 and (with Woodhorn Colliery Museum) plates 4, 6, 7, 9, 11, 16, 17, 20: Pamela Gorman and the late John Gorman, the illustration on page 19: Tyne and Wear Archives Service, the illustration on page 14: William Ward, the illustrations on pages 1 and 45: Woodhorn Colliery Museum, plates 1–3, 5, 8, 10, 12–15, 18, 19 and 22–27.

LOCATIONS OF THE BANNERS

The banners in this catalogue are held at Woodhorn Colliery Museum, QE2 Country Park, Ashington, Northumberland, NE63 9VF, unless otherwise noted in the list of illustrations. The Museum is able to display only five banners at a time, but it does have photographic records of *all* the surviving Northumberland miners' banners which can be viewed by prior arrangement. Access to those banners not held at the Museum must be sought through the relevant institutions.

Another Northumberland miners' banner has been discovered but too late to be included in any detail in this book. This banner represents the Backworth Federated Group of Miners' Lodges Welfare Scheme and hangs in the Backworth Miners' Welfare Centre. It is a post-nationalization banner made by Tutill, Chesham.

PRIMARY SOURCES

Unless otherwise stated these sources are held at Northumberland Record Office, Morpeth Record Centre, Northumberland:
Annual Northumberland Miners' Picnic Sub-committee Minute-Books, 1919–63
Ashington Mineworkers' Federation Minute-Books, 1925–49
Bedlington 'A' Branch Minute-Books, 1948–55
Burradon Branch Minute-Books, 1931–67
Ellington Branch Minute-Books (held by NUM, Northumberland Area)
George Tutill catalogue, May 1885 (held at Beamish, the North of England Open Air Museum)
Pegswood Branch Minute-Books, 1916–64
Seghill Branch Minute-Books, 1946–60
Sleekburn Branch Minute-Books, 1930–70
Woodhorn Branch Minute-Books, 1912–81

BANNER COLLECTIONS CONSULTED

National Coal Mining Museum for England, Wakefield, Yorkshire
National Union of Mineworkers, Durham Area, Durham
National Museum of Labour History, Manchester
Woodhorn Colliery Museum, Ashington, Northumberland

SELECT BIBLIOGRAPHY

Bellamy, J., 'Trade union imagery', *The Open University, Arts Foundation Course A102*, 1986

Campbell, T. & Wilson, M., *Each for All and All for Each; a celebration of co-operative banners*, National Co-operative Education Association, 1994

Cooper, E., *People's Art: working class art from 1750 to the present day*, Edinburgh: Mainstream Publishing, 1994

Davison, J., *Northumberland Miners 1919–39*, NUM Northumberland Area, 1973

Dunn, P., 'Trade union banners as a source of Labour history', *Modern History Review*, Vol. 7, No. 1, September 1995

Feaver, W., *Pitmen Painters: the Ashington Group, 1934–1984*, London: Chatto and Windus, 1988; reprinted Ashington/Manchester: MidNAG/Carcanet Press, 1993

Fynes, R., *The Miners of Northumberland and Durham: a history of their social and political progress*, 1873; republished Newcastle upon Tyne: Davis Books, 1986

Gorman, J., *Images of Labour: selected memorabilia from the National Museum of Labour History*, Buckhurst Hill, Essex: Scorpion Publishing Limited, 1985

Gorman, J., *Banner Bright: an illustrated history of trade union banners*, Buckhurst Hill, Essex: Scorpion Publishing Limited, 1986

Hall, J., *Dictionary of Subjects and Symbols in Art*, London: John Murray, 1974

Kirkup, M., *The Biggest Mining Village in the World: a social history of Ashington*, Warkworth, Northumberland: Sandhill Press, 1993

Leeson, R.A., *United We Stand: an illustrated account of trade union emblems*, Bath: Adams and Dart, 1971

Lewery, A.J., *Popular Art Past and Present*, Newton Abbot, Devon: David and Charles, 1991

Moyes, W.A., *Banner Parade: a selection of lodge banners of the Durham Miners' Association*, Newcastle upon Tyne: Frank Graham, 1973

Moyes, W.A., *The Banner Book: a study of the banners of the lodges of Durham Miners' Association*, Newcastle upon Tyne: Frank Graham, 1974

Tuck, J., *The Collieries of Northumberland Volume 1*, Newcastle upon Tyne: Trade Union Printing Services, 1993

Tuck, J., *The Collieries of Northumberland Volume 2*, Newcastle upon Tyne: Trade Union Printing Services, 1995

Williams, D. & Muirhead, G., *Northumberland Miners' Banners*, Ashington, Northumberland: Mid Northumberland Arts Group, 1987

PLATE 1
Ashington Group of Collieries (front)

PLATE 2
Ashington Group of Collieries (back)

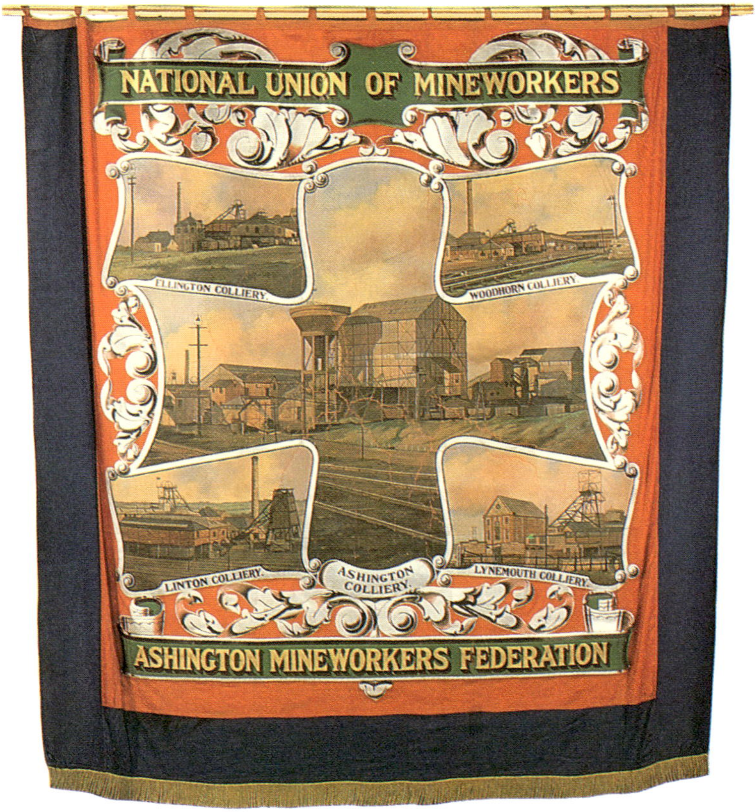

PLATE 3
Ashington Mineworkers' Federation, 1950s (front)

PLATE 4
Ashington Mineworkers' Federation, 1940s (back)

PLATE 5
Ashington Mineworkers' Federation, 1950s (back)

PLATE 6
Bomarsund (front)

PLATE 7
Bomarsund (back)

PLATE 8
Brenkley and
Seaton Burn (front)

PLATE 9
Burradon and Weetslade (front)

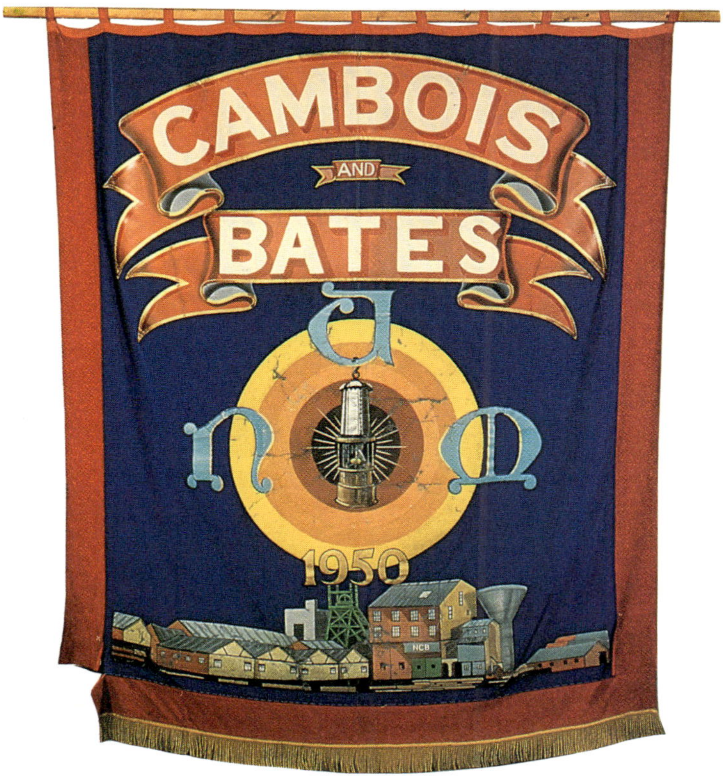

PLATE 10
Cambois and Bates (front)

PLATE 11
Doctor Pit,
Bedlington (front)

PLATE 12
Dudley (front)

PLATE 13
Ellington (front)

PLATE 14
Ellington (back)

PLATE 15
Lynemouth (front)

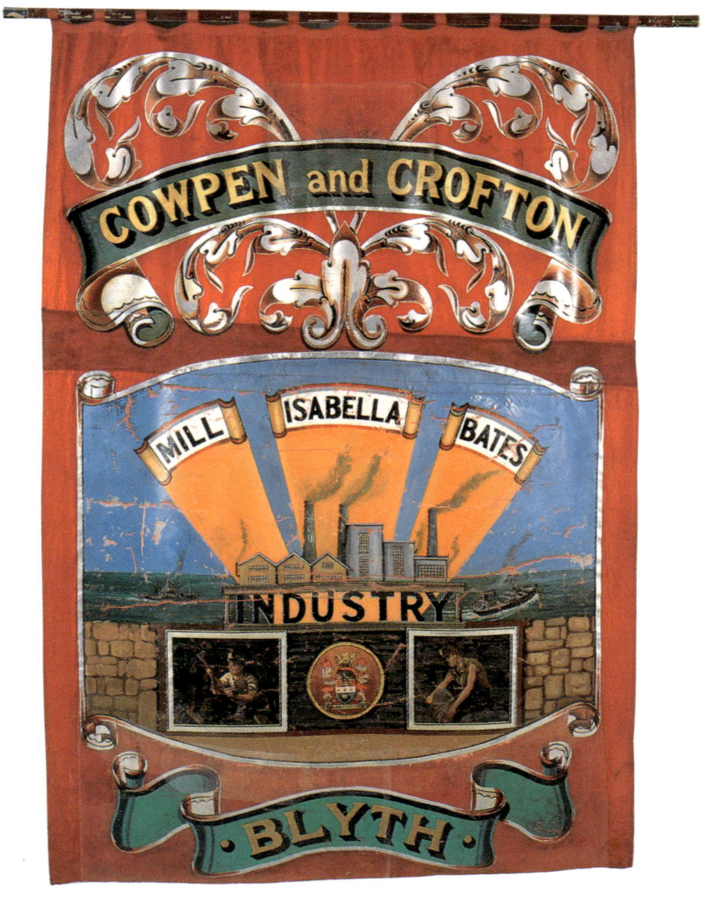

PLATE 16
Mill, Isabella, Bates (front)

PLATE 17
North Seaton
(front)

PLATE 18
North Walbottle
(front)

PLATE 19
North Walbottle
(back)

PLATE 20
Pegswood (front)

PLATE 21
Pegswood (back)

PLATE 22
Rising Sun,
Wallsend (front)

PLATE 23
Seghill (front)

PLATE 24
Sleekburn 'A'
(front)

PLATE 25
West Sleekburn
(front)

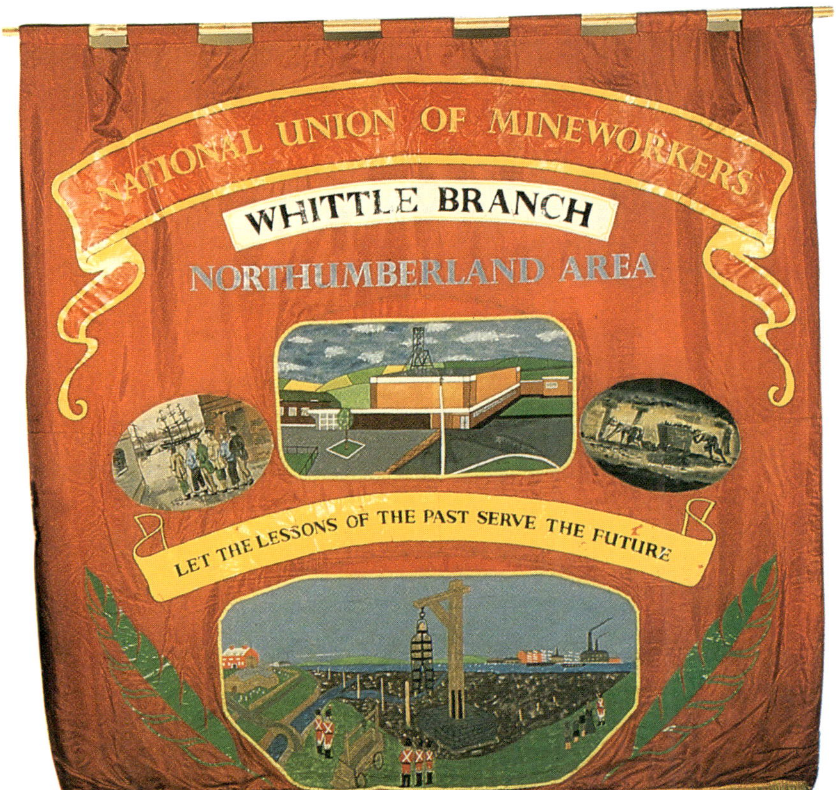

PLATE 26
Whittle (back)

PLATE 27
Woodhorn (front)